The Inner Confidence Factor Workbook

The Inner Confidence Factor

IMPORTANT

The Inner Confidence Factor must not be used as "treatment" for any mental health condition.

If you have, or believe that you may have, mental health issues, please make an appointment with you health practitioner for professional support.

"Subtle changes...

...lead to powerful results"

The Elements That Contribute To Confidence

There are ten elements that you could use or practice to help you feel more confidence.

Acceptance

Self-care

Body language

Role play

Values

THE ELEMENTS

Trust

Preparation & practice

Visualization

Breathing

self-talk

However, that doesn't mean you have to incorporate every single one of the elements into your life—you can pick and choose whatever works best for you.

You may decide that certain elements work better for specific situations, or that one is a great fit for everything.

One thing to bare in mind, however, is the elements' different levels of importance.

While they're all useful in helping you to feel more confident, this book will focus on only four of the elements...

1

2

3

4

Values
Trust
Self-talk
Acceptance

Put it this way, you *could* practice all the other elements: self care, body language, role play, visualization, breathing, and preparation and practice, but the confidence you'll feel won't ever be as deep.

As an example, some women's self-care may consist of things like reading a book, spending quality time with family or friends, having a massage, going for a walk, or taking a bath with some essential oils and candles.

Doing those things may boost her confidence, but if she still talks negatively to herself, and consistently gets upset with herself for doing it, she'll undo all her good work every time.

Why?

Because the four elements above form your *internal* self-care, which is just as, if not more important than, external self-care.

So these four will be the focus of this book because they alone will make a huge difference in your life over time.

What Areas Need Attention?

Before you continue, it would be good for you to get an idea of what areas need your attention the most.

There might be multiple areas in your life where you don't feel as confident as you'd like to feel but instead of focusing on all areas, it might be easier to start with one or two. That way, you'll reduce the chance of feeling overwhelmed.

You might, on the other hand, prefer more of a go-with-the-flow approach and not focus on any specific area. This approach lends itself extremely well to the four elements.

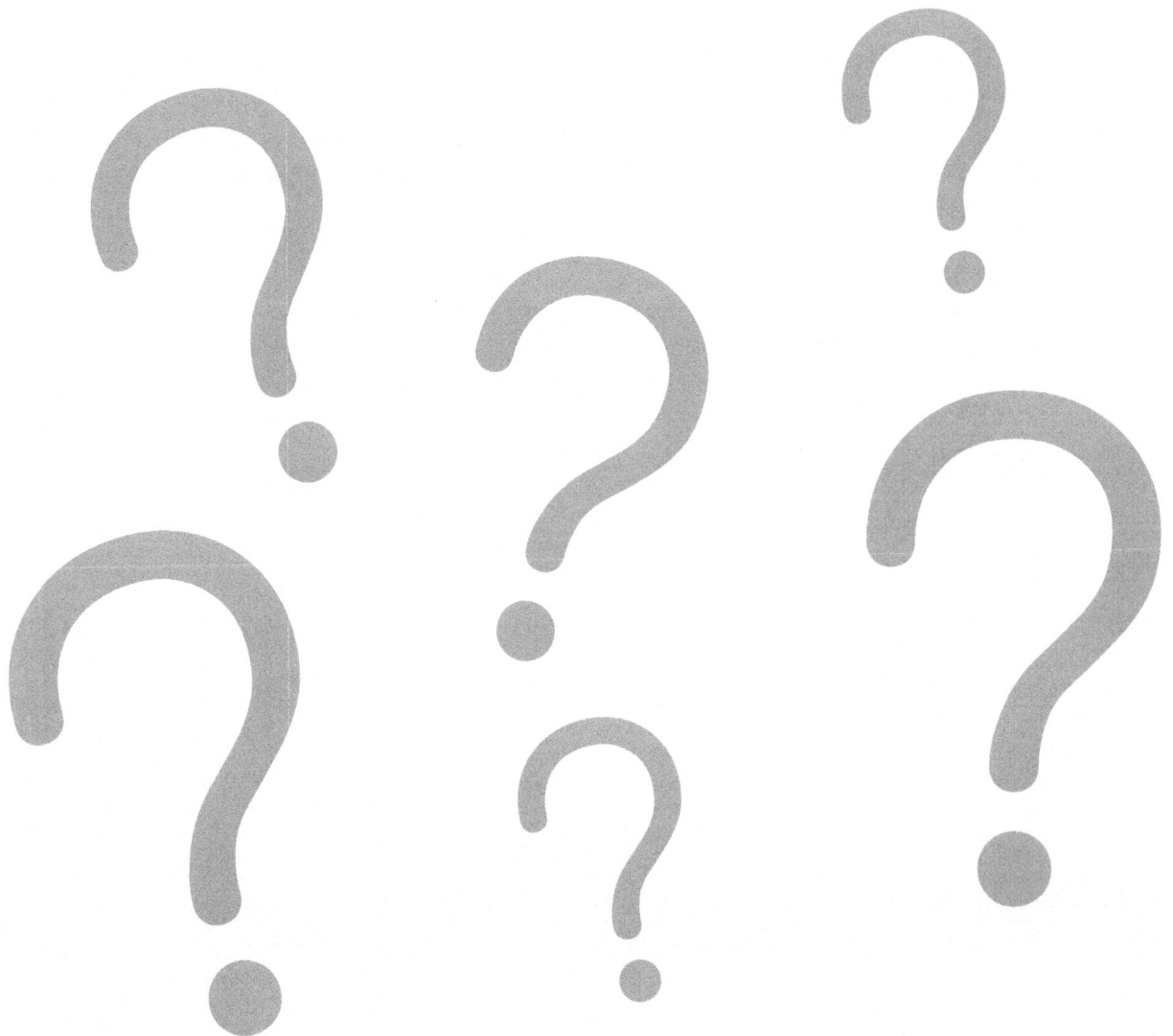

To help you figure out the areas you need help with, you can go through the confidence assessment. All you'll need to do is rate each statement on a scale of 1–5:

1   Never/no/no way!

2   I'd feel a lot of anxiety/uncomfortable. It would take a lot of effort to do/go for it (better if I'm with someone)

3   I would still feel a bit anxious/uncomfortable/find it difficult, so only occasionally

4   I wouldn't necessarily enjoy it/find it easy but can do it

5   Absolutely!

The aim of this assessment is to help you see where you're starting from, and going through this book will help you to increase your lowest scores.

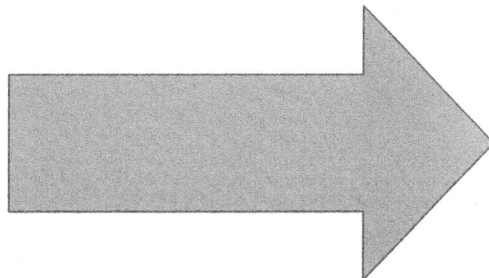

The Confidence Assessment

1 - Never/no/no way!
2 - I'd feel a lot of anxiety/uncomfortable & it would take a lot of effort to do/go for it (even better if I'm with someone)
3 - I would still feel a bit anxious/uncomfortable/find it difficult, so only occasionally
4 - I wouldn't necessarily enjoy it/find it easy but can do it
5 - Absolutely!

I initiate conversations with strangers	1 - 2 - 3 - 4 - 5
I initiate conversations with people I know	1 - 2 - 3 - 4 - 5
I talk about my interests/passions//hobbies to new people openly	1 - 2 - 3 - 4 - 5
I make consistent eye contact in conversation with new people	1 - 2 - 3 - 4 - 5
I make consistent eye contact in conversation with people I know	1 - 2 - 3 - 4 - 5
I ask questions in conversations with people I don't know	1 - 2 - 3 - 4 - 5
I smile at strangers first	1 - 2 - 3 - 4 - 5
I give compliments to strangers	1 - 2 - 3 - 4 - 5
I give compliments to people I know	1 - 2 - 3 - 4 - 5
I let people know I need time to think if I don't have an immediate answer to their question	1 - 2 - 3 - 4 - 5
I reciprocate when people I don't know talk to me	1 - 2 - 3 - 4 - 5
I ask for directions if I'm lost	1 - 2 - 3 - 4 - 5

1 - Never/no/no way!
2 - I'd feel a lot of anxiety/uncomfortable & it would take a lot of effort to do/go for it (even better if I'm with someone)
3 - I would still feel a bit anxious/uncomfortable/find it difficult, so only occasionally
4 - I wouldn't necessarily enjoy it/find it easy but can do it
5 - Absolutely!

I trust myself to make good decisions	1 - 2 - 3 - 4 - 5
I take on new challenges	1 - 2 - 3 - 4 - 5
I look at myself naked in the mirror	1 - 2 - 3 - 4 - 5
I accept compliments	1 - 2 - 3 - 4 - 5
I let people I know see the real me	1 - 2 - 3 - 4 - 5
I let people I don't know see the real me	1 - 2 - 3 - 4 - 5
I say no to the things I genuinely don't want to do	1 - 2 - 3 - 4 - 5
I give my opinion, even if I don't think anyone will agree with me	1 - 2 - 3 - 4 - 5
I let people know when they have stepped out of line	1 - 2 - 3 - 4 - 5
I stand up for myself	1 - 2 - 3 - 4 - 5
I walk with my head up and shoulders back/with purpose	1 - 2 - 3 - 4 - 5
I go to public places, like bars/cafes/networking events, alone	1 - 2 - 3 - 4 - 5

Now that you've been through the assessment, you should have a clear indication of the areas to focus on. If you'd rather focus on something else or you have, say, mainly ones and twos across the entire assessment, just choose and start with the area you feel would benefit you the most right now.

How Do I feel About My Results?

Who Do You Want to Be?

You wouldn't be holding this workbook in your hands if you didn't want to make some changes in your life, but are you clear on what you really want? What does confidence look like to _you_?

How one person views confidence might not be the same as you. So let's consider who and how you want to be when you have deep, inner confidence.

Answer the next few questions to help you get clear on what you're aiming for so that you can use your answers as a measure of your progress.

How do you feel when you wake up in the morning?

How do you feel and what do you do when you have free time and you're alone?

How do you feel and what do you do when meeting new people?

How do you respond when faced with a challenge(s)?

What's your body language like when you enter an unfamiliar public space?

How do you respond to compliments?

What are you like 1:1 with a person?

What are you like when you're in a group of people?

How do you feel about making changes in your life that fit who you are?

How do you respond to harsh criticism/judgment?

What do you do when you make mistakes?

How do you talk to yourself?

Get Clear on Your Values

We all have values, but unfortunately many of us don't live by them.

Another thing is that even though we have them, we may not be tuned into them, so we end up feeling frustrated and disappointed because we consistently do things that don't match what really matters to us.

Getting clear on your values will help you to get clear on the things you want to say yes to and the things you'd rather say no to, but there may certainly be some exceptions.

For example, let's say you're in a job you hate because it sells a product you don't even like and would never use. You would never recommend it to anyone, yet there you are working in the finance department making sure the numbers add up and that the company continues to make a healthy profit.

You may not be able to immediately give your notice and walk away, but at least getting clear on your values in the area of work/career will help you to understand what matters the most to you, and from there you can take the necessary steps to eventually move out of that job and into something that you're more likely to enjoy.

So with that said, let's get you clear on your values in different areas of your life.

We're going to look at six areas:

- Work/career
- Business
- Family
- Social/friends
- Love/romance
- Health/fitness

You certainly don't have to be in a relationship to go through the love/romance section; you can simply base it on how you would *like* a relationship to be.

And remember, love can also pertain to the relationship you have with yourself—something to keep in mind.

Also, you may not have a business, so if that's the case, skip that section.

What Are Your Values?

Thinking about the following areas of your life, write down your top 3–5 values for each of the following areas (you may have more, but let's just go with 3–5):

Work/Career   Rating

_____   _____

_____   _____

_____   _____

_____   _____

_____   _____

Business

_____   _____

_____   _____

_____   _____

_____   _____

_____   _____

Family

_____   _____

_____   _____

_____   _____

_____   _____

_____   _____

Social/Friends

_____

Rating

_____

_____   _____

_____   _____

_____   _____

_____   _____

Love/Romance

_____

_____   _____

_____   _____

_____   _____

_____   _____

Health/Fitness

_____

_____   _____

_____   _____

_____   _____

_____   _____

Now, a question for you...

Are all of the values you've written down really *your* values?

When we were growing up, well meaning people: parents, teachers and other adults passed many of their beliefs on to us, and being innocent children, and then looking for guidance and direction as we grew older, we believed many of those beliefs and took them on as our own without question.

As adults, we develop some of our own ideas and beliefs but may also still be hanging on to what was passed on to us.

You know what happens when you have a belief, don't you?
You live in accordance with whatever it is you believe to be true, for the most part.

Another thing is that some of us are also still trying to make someone from years ago proud (or prove something to that person), whether we're consciously aware of it or not. There's nothing wrong with that if it's doing you good, but if it's leading to frustration and disappointment, because you don't really want to do whatever you're doing, then it's a problem.

So, could you be holding on to values that aren't your own?

Go back and take a look again at what you wrote down for each category and give each value a rating on a scale of 1–10. 10 means it's 100% important and 1 means not at all.

But before you do the exercise, please bear this in mind...

You're not putting them in order of importance; you're looking at each value in *isolation* and asking yourself, "how *genuinely* important is this specific value to me on a scale of 1—10?"

Go back to do the exercise before moving on!

The whole point of getting you to rate your values is that if you've given anything less than a 10, then you have to ask yourself why.

If something is really important to you, then it's important, period.

There won't be any ifs, buts, or maybes, and there's unlikely to be any 1–9 scores. You may put them in a certain order as to say, "I would put this before this," but they would all still have a 10 rating.

Make sense?

If you're thinking, "but there *are* some that are more important than others to me," that's okay. It's not that you wouldn't or shouldn't list them in a specific order—you can still do that—but because it's something that's highly important to you, it will still be a 10.

And this is about the things that mean *everything* to you, so if you now realize that some of them aren't your values, or if you've given some of them a rating lower than 10, feel free to put them aside for now and focus on your 10s.

Have you given any less than 10?

Build Trust in Yourself

For most of us, we don't trust anyone right away; it's something that has to be earned. It's unfortunate because it would be nice to know that everyone has your back, whether you know them or not, but it just doesn't work that way.

When it comes to trusting yourself, the questions is, do you? Do you trust yourself a little, a lot, or not at all? And this can be in any area of your life. It may be that you trust yourself to take good care of your children (if you have any) or to do the really simple things like make a cup of tea.

You may trust your ability to do a good job at work or in your business because you know exactly what to do and how to do it. But what about all the other areas in which you're a bit wobbly?

The areas in which you procrastinate, or maybe you just back out of something because you don't trust yourself to do a good job, get something right or handle a situation.

Then, there are the times when we hear that little voice that tells us what to do, and what do we do? We ignore it. A bit later on, we then find ourselves saying, "I knew it!" or "why didn't I just do what I thought to do in the first place?"

So what can you do to start the process of trusting yourself more often? Practice.

There's no other way because it's not as if you're going to go from not trusting to trusting overnight.

If it were that easy, you would've done it by now, don't you think?

So practice it is, and the good thing is, you can take tiny steps to begin with, and as you get more and more use to following that voice and trusting yourself, you can take things up a notch, whatever that may be for you.

Something else to consider is that that we don't always get a little voice speaking to us. It can often come in the form of a feeling. But we may still ignore it.

So whether it's a voice or a feeling, you're going to start getting that practice in.

You're now going to be asked to do three things. Don't worry, it won't be anything weird. All you need to do is follow along.

1 - The first thing you're going to do is think of something that:

- You don't want to do, but you know it needs to be done
- Will take less than five minutes to do
- Is preferably something you can do within the next ten to twenty minutes or so

Now, read out the following to yourself:

I promise to take action on (whatever you've decided to do). This is a contract with myself, and I refuse to break it.

I'm getting this done today!

Name: _____

Signed: _____

2 - Now, you're going to think about something you're having difficulty making a decision about. Something that preferably has two possible options.

Next, you'll need to take a coin. Any size will do, and you're going to toss it. Heads means one option, and tails, the other.

It might seem strange or silly using a coin to make a decision for you, but if you're struggling between two options, then let something else do it for you, and that will be it: decision made.

So, decide which side represents which, do your best to put aside any thoughts of "this is silly," focus on whatever you've chosen to focus on, and go for it before moving on: toss that coin!

Presuming you've now done that, what's really important is not knowing what side the coin landed on, but how you **felt** when it landed.

So for example, did you feel excited and happy? Did you want to jump for joy? Maybe it was a combination. Maybe you felt scared but excited.

Or did you feel a sense of dread? Did you have a sinking feeling?

Tuning in to what you *felt* will give you a stronger indication of what you really want to do instead of relying on a coin to make the decision for you (unless you really do want it to).

So, as long as you've been honest about what you felt, you should now have a clearer answer.

But maybe you didn't feel anything but found yourself *hoping* that it would fall on a certain side. That "hoping" will also tell you what you *really* want.

Either way, with your clear answer, you can now weigh up the pros and cons with a clear head instead of trying to do it while "you don't know," which won't help you to feel secure and trust in any final decision you make.

What you're going to do now is think about something else you've been avoiding doing for a while and think about the reason *why* you're avoiding it.

Sometimes, we avoid or hold back from doing things because we believe that we won't be able to handle the outcome of doing that thing.

There might be a "worst case scenario" we keep picturing over and over again, which leads to the avoidance. It could be something as simple as being bored to death or, something that most people fear, being ridiculed.

So today, you're going to "go there."

You're going to actually think about this worst case scenario again, but this time, you're going to consider how you would or could handle the situation *if* that worst case scenario were to play out.

At this point, You might be thinking, "but I really won't be able to handle it," so think back to a time when you had a challenge in your life that you thought you wouldn't get through or handle, but you did. There's probably many times that come to mind.

Use *that* as proof.

Proof that yes, it may be challenging, and you might feel worried, uncertain, or scared, but you *absolutely can handle it.*

And that's what you're reminding yourself by thinking about that worst case scenario and writing down how you'll get through it. This is you trusting yourself to handle whatever arises.

So, consider what you *think* would happen, write it down and then write out everything that comes to mind around how you could or would deal with it.

What I'm Avoiding	How I Can Handle the Situation

Now, there's something you haven't yet done.

Remember that promise you made to yourself? Your "contract." You're going to do it now.

If you genuinely can't do it now because something important has come up, get a sticky note and write down <u>exactly when</u> you're going to take action on your promise.

Remember, you made this promise to yourself. It's your contract and you signed it.

If you don't act on it, you're simply doing the opposite of what this section was all about. You're proving to yourself that you can't trust yourself.

Either do it now or write down the time, preferably **within the next 24 hours,** that you're *definitely* going to do it.

I'm doing it now!

This is when I will definitely do it:

_____

Accept Difficult Situations

Many of us are walking around in resistance. Resistance to things like our circumstances, events, and people.

What we don't realize is that the resistance we feel is what makes our life ten times harder and a lot less enjoyable.

If you can start feeling more acceptance of what is as opposed to wishing something wasn't a certain way, wishing it would stop, or just go away, you'll free up energy, which can then be directed elsewhere.

Having said that, this isn't about about giving up, feeling hopeless, and making do. Some things you really can't change. and some things you can. Here are a couple quick examples.

One thing you can't change is people judging you harshly. You might be able to change some people's negative opinions about you, other people, or the world but the rest, no chance. If you're someone who always gets upset about people judging, do you realize that this will always drag you down? Do you realize that wanting people to *stop* judging is a waste of your energy? This is simply because, whether you like it or not, you have no control over what most people say and how they act, and that includes whether you know them or not.

The second example is to do with frustration.

How do you feel when you get frustrated? Do you feel uncomfortable? Do you want to stop feeling frustrated as quickly as possible? Do you sometimes get annoyed or even more frustrated that you're feeling frustrated in the first place?

For most people, feeling frustrated does not feel good, and if you're someone who dislikes the feeling and tries to get rid of it, there's a strong chance that you end up feeling worse.

Now, if the frustration is to do with, say, a job you don't enjoy, you can do something about it. You can start looking for another job or look to start your own business.

The only things is, while you're planning to leave that position at some point, the frustration you feel remains, so how can you accept that which doesn't feel good?

Here's an exercise for you to practice.

It's not necessarily an easy one, but the more you do it, the more you'll feel the benefits, and the more you'll be able to handle acceptance of challenging situations.

Try this exercise. Think of an everyday situation in which you always feel frustrated.

Close your eyes and think about that situation. And as you feel the feeling of frustration arising in your body, notice **where** you're feeling it the most. It won't feel great, but do your best to stick with it.

What you're then going to do for the next minute is simply follow the feeling. You're not trying to stop it, push it away, or even ignore it. You're letting it be there.

Have a go now before moving on.

How did that go? Did you feel the frustration lessen, even if it were only a little?

Did you notice how, even though the feeling is uncomfortable, it was easier to simply sit with it than fight against or resist it?

If you still felt as though you wanted it to stop and you were trying to "get rid" of the feeling, that's okay. What you'll find, though, is that as you practice sitting with whatever feeling is coming up for you, the better you get at it.

But you're not aiming for perfection. You're human after all, but at least you know that you don't have to be at the mercy of your emotions. And please don't think you need to be emotionless and not cry or show anger, etc.

The ultimate goal of this exercise is to help you move toward a place where you don't make yourself wrong for having certain feelings that you don't think you should be having, and that you ultimately feel more in control.

At this point, it's important to make it clear that acceptance *does not* mean being a doormat and allowing people to walk all over you. It's not about shrugging your shoulders toward crimes or justifying anyone's unkind or cruel behavior.

You may feel angry, disgusted, disappointed, sad, frustrated, exhausted, etc. Whatever you feel, it's about accepting that you can't control everything that happens in the world and understanding that resisting the way you feel makes that feeling stick around longer; therefore, you'll feel worse for longer.

It's about doing your best to protect your sanity and well-being.

So when you stop fighting and resisting against things in the world you can't change, it leaves you free to get on with your life and reuse the saved energy differently and in a way that's useful to you. And when you stop fighting and resisting against the way you feel, the feeling tends to dissipate a lot quicker.

If there's something you can change, then do what you need to do to change it, but you'll be much more effective at it when you're not expending unnecessary energy.

This exercise isn't a magic solution (or maybe it will be, who knows), but it's much better than any kind of quick fix "solution" you may want to try.

Last, if you ever feel bad for feeling bad, try asking the following questions:

What if I chose to not make myself wrong for feeling this way?

You can also ask:

What am I resisting? Or
What if I stopped resisting this feeling?

If one way isn't working to help you feel better, you might as well try something else!

Supportive Self-talk

How many times have you mentally "beat" yourself up this week? Whether it's one time or hundreds, it hasn't helped has it? How many times have you been unkind toward yourself and immediately felt better? Never, probably.

We know deep down that we're not helping ourselves; that it doesn't do us any good, but we keep doing it. There's also the chance that what we say to ourselves is not necessarily what we really think; we just heard it from someone else, and we end up repeating it over and over again and manage to convince ourselves that it's true.

Ultimately, whether it's someone else's words or your own, it doesn't matter. The fact is, the harsh words you repeat to yourself every day are doing nothing to support you in feeling good about yourself and helping you to feel more confident and capable.

The thing about it, though, is that you're never going to be able to stop thinking, unless you meditate permanently. So how can you stop all the self-bashing?

What if you didn't necessarily have to stop those voices?

What if it were easier to let them be there instead of spending energy on trying to change them?

You might be thinking, "but I feel bad when I speak harshly toward myself, and I don't want to do it anymore," so consider the *why* behind that. What makes you feel bad about what you say to yourself? What makes you see it as a problem?

Could it possibly be because a part of you worries that all the harsh things you say to yourself could be true?

When you think about it, you don't get upset or feel bad if someone says something to you that you don't believe. If someone called you a pink bottle of water, you're hardly likely to feel hurt.

So *why* do you feel bad?

Whatever your answer, this goes back to the last section on accepting challenging situations because the unkind way you talk to yourself *is* challenging. It may feel difficult for you to know how to deal with it and there's likely to be a lot of resistance around the fact that you actually do it.

So this is a good opportunity for you to put into practice the last section. In other words, practice sitting with the things you say to yourself. Observe them instead of judging the words you use and yourself for saying them.

And here's some good news for you, when you allow your thoughts to flow, more and more will keep coming until that critical voice disappears, almost like getting washed away.

But still, it would be useful to have some supportive words for yourself alongside practicing acceptance of what is. That way, you have more than one thing you can do.

So now, on the lines below, you're going to write down up to four unsupportive things you often say to or about yourself.

"_____"

"_____"

"_____"

"_____"

Now, reading through what you've written, consider how you would respond if someone you cared about said those exact same things about herself in front of you. Someone who mattered to you a great deal.

What would you say to that person?

Write your responses in the boxes below:

Last, whatever you've just written down, you're now going to read through it again, but this time, replace "you" with "I", "me," or "myself."

If what you wrote is specific to a particular person, you might need to change the wording a little so that it makes more sense.

After you've read each one, simply say a heartfelt "thank you'" and then sit with it for a few seconds.

Do that now, and if you feel any discomfort, just keep in mind the section on acceptance.

Next, three questions...

1. What or who makes you laugh?
2. Who can you **easily** ignore no matter what they say, especially when it's something negative?
3. And who do you trust and admire the most?

You might have a cartoon character in mind, a relative, a celebrity or even a... politician.

If you can imagine someone you can easily ignore saying the harsh things to you that you say to yourself, you're more likely to roll your eyes and think "oh go away" and dismiss the words more easily, so they won't have the same effect on you.

On the other hand, if it were a cartoon character with a funny voice saying those harsh things, you'd probably laugh at some point and again, not feel anywhere near as bad.

Give it a go with one or two of your unsupportive comments you wrote down and see how different it feels before continuing...

When it comes to the person you admire, imagine that person saying positive things about you or to you. How would you feel then?

Because you trust what that person says, you're more likely to listen and believe the words, and *that* will change how you feel. It will help those more positive comments to sink in and have a positive effect on you rather than you simply thinking them or reading them aloud and trying to force yourself to believe them.

Take one of your positive comments and imagine that person saying it to you. What do you feel this time?

_____

There's one last thing you can do: write a supportive letter to your future self.

You can use this type of exercise to help you see how far you've come, or it can act as a great reminder to get you back on track.

Type "write a letter to my future self" in Google and there will be plenty of websites where you can do this, or you can write yourself a physical letter.

The latter option might mean you would have to "hide" it somewhere for you to find at a later date or hand it to someone trustworthy who would be willing to hold it for you and post it at an appropriate time. You might even decide to hang on to it and read it weekly, monthly, or however often you wish.

If you choose to do this, here are some examples of prompts you could use if you're unsure of how to start.

- I'm writing you to remind you that _____
- It's OK to _____
- Sometimes you'll forget to _____ but that doesn't mean _____
- You are more _____ than you realize because _____
- You deserve to _____
- You don't need to _____

Now that you've completed the Inner Confidence Factor, you're going to bring it all together in a simple way...

Bringing it All Together

Values

You've now identified your most important values, and you know that they're 100% your **own**, so your next step is to ensure that your life starts to move more and more in the direction of those values.

Choose one area of your life, and write down one thing you're going to tweak, change or eradicate so that this particular area of your life matches—just that little bit more—what's important to you. Over time, you can make more changes but for now, one will do.

I'm going to tweak, change or eradicate...

_____

_____

_____

_____

_____

_____

_____

_____

_____

Build Trust in Yourself

To keep building up on your levels of self-trust, you can simply keep practicing. You don't have to do anything big if you don't want to, just give yourself little things to do, make that promise to yourself, sign the "contract" and then do it.

Over time, you can move on to bigger and bigger things.

For now, write down *when* you're going to tweak, change or eradicate that one thing in your life and make your promise statement based on that, either your own or the one you read out in the trust section.

Write down any "worst case scenarios" that may come to mind when you think about making the changes and then write out how you would or could deal with the situation should it arise.

_____

_____

_____

_____

_____

_____

_____

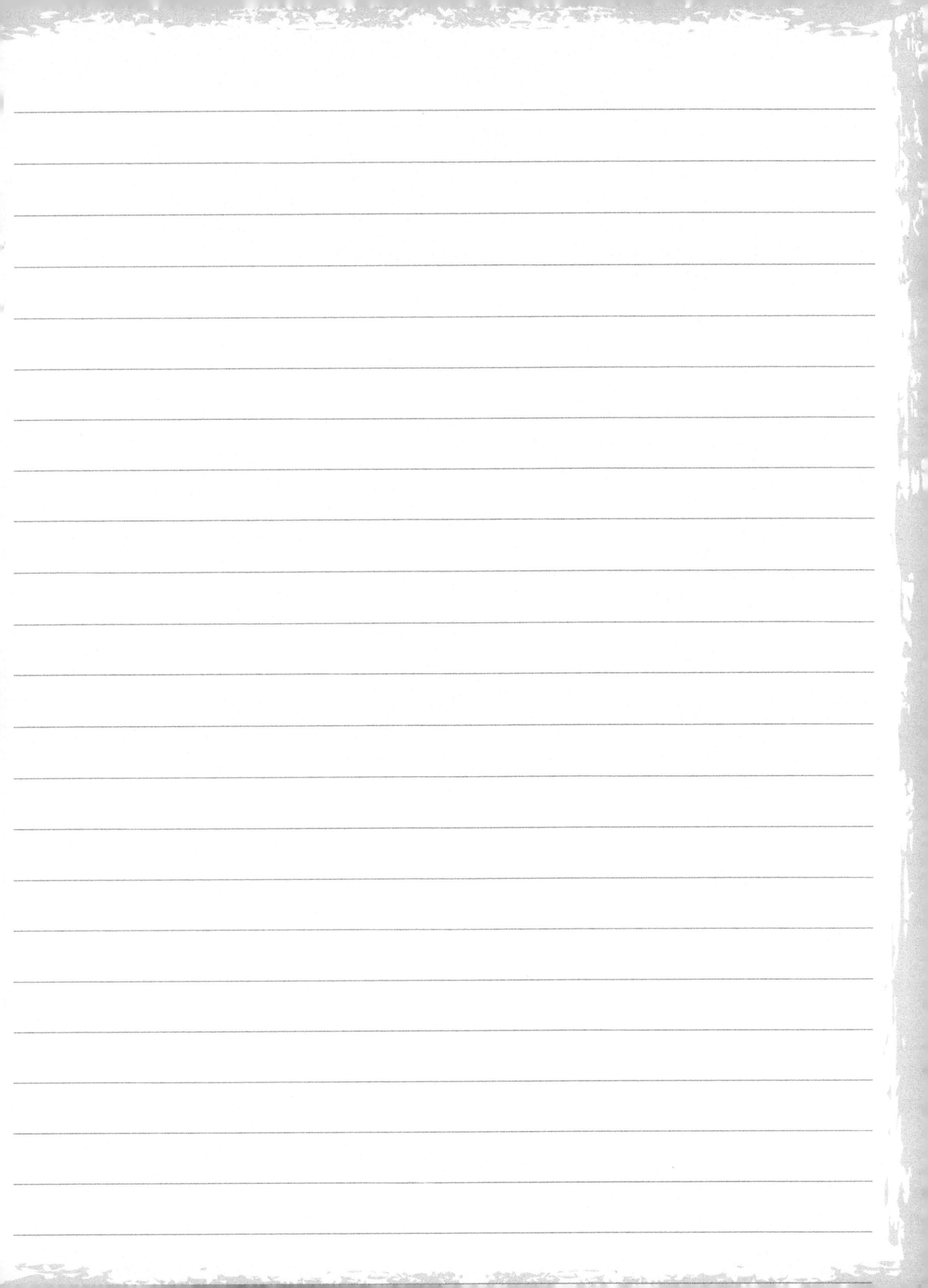

Acceptance

Acceptance is a challenging one but worth practicing, and it's highly effective in helping you to stay more relaxed and not let any thoughts or feelings get to you so much.

As a reminder, it's not about resigning yourself to not doing something that can be done about a situation. It's about accepting the *reality* of that situation and the way you're feeling or thinking in any given moment and not letting any of it get in the way and deplete your energy.

Think about any negative, unhelpful, or scary thoughts you're having around that thing you've chosen to tweak, change, or eradicate and just sit with them for a few minutes, maybe two or three to start, and feel how the way you feel changes.

Self-talk

Remember the person you thought of who you respect and admire?

Imagine that person supporting the change you've decided to make.

What words of encouragement would that person use to make sure you really do it and that you don't put it off until it's forgotten?

Write out a paragraph of that person's words, read it through and say one last *heartfelt* "thank you."

_____

_____

_____

_____

_____

_____

_____

_____

_____

So, how do you feel right now?

Whatever your answer, this workbook is a starting point; it wasn't designed to be an overnight quick-fix solution.

It was designed for you to start feeling positive changes within yourself right from the start, and it's also about pointing you in a direction that, if you continue to follow, will enable you to feel deeper levels of confidence over time.

The four elements of acceptance, self-talk, values, and trust may not be anything new, and they may not seem all that "sexy," let's say, but keep nurturing and practicing them and you *will* reap the benefits.

That doesn't mean you will feel confident 100% of the time. You're human, and life can be incredibly challenging sometimes, so on the days that feel difficult, the four elements will, at the very least, help you to cope.

And remember, you're not trying to prove to anyone how confident you are or can be, you're doing this for yourself and yourself alone, and as you do this for yourself, people around you will also benefit in some way.

In other words, it's a win for everyone.

What 3 positive things do you want to say to yourself right now for going through and getting to the end of this workbook?

Say them out loud, in your head and/or write them down, it's your choice.

1.

2.

3.

Confidence Tracker Chart — Track Your Progress!

Rate your level of confidence on a scale of 1–10 every day to build a visual picture of your progress. But don't "kick" yourself if the chart doesn't look how you want it to look. Progress isn't linear!

	MON	TUE	WED	THUR	FRI	SAT	SUN
10	○	○	○	○	○	○	○
9	○	○	○	○	○	○	○
8	○	○	○	○	○	○	○
7	○	○	○	○	○	○	○
6	○	○	○	○	○	○	○
5	○	○	○	○	○	○	○
4	○	○	○	○	○	○	○
3	○	○	○	○	○	○	○
2	○	○	○	○	○	○	○
1	○	○	○	○	○	○	○

Confidence Tracker Chart — Track Your Progress!

Rate your level of confidence on a scale of 1–10 every day to build a visual picture of your progress. But don't "kick" yourself if the chart doesn't look how you want it to look. Progress isn't linear!

	MON	TUE	WED	THUR	FRI	SAT	SUN
10	○	○	○	○	○	○	○
9	○	○	○	○	○	○	○
8	○	○	○	○	○	○	○
7	○	○	○	○	○	○	○
6	○	○	○	○	○	○	○
5	○	○	○	○	○	○	○
4	○	○	○	○	○	○	○
3	○	○	○	○	○	○	○
2	○	○	○	○	○	○	○
1	○	○	○	○	○	○	○

Confidence Tracker Chart — Track Your Progress!

Rate your level of confidence on a scale of 1–10 every day to build a visual picture of your progress. But don't "kick" yourself if the chart doesn't look how you want it to look. Progress isn't linear!

	MON	TUE	WED	THUR	FRI	SAT	SUN
10	○	○	○	○	○	○	○
9	○	○	○	○	○	○	○
8	○	○	○	○	○	○	○
7	○	○	○	○	○	○	○
6	○	○	○	○	○	○	○
5	○	○	○	○	○	○	○
4	○	○	○	○	○	○	○
3	○	○	○	○	○	○	○
2	○	○	○	○	○	○	○
1	○	○	○	○	○	○	○

Confidence Tracker Chart — Track Your Progress!

Rate your level of confidence on a scale of 1–10 every day to build a visual picture of your progress. But don't "kick" yourself if the chart doesn't look how you want it to look. Progress isn't linear!

	MON	TUE	WED	THUR	FRI	SAT	SUN
10	○	○	○	○	○	○	○
9	○	○	○	○	○	○	○
8	○	○	○	○	○	○	○
7	○	○	○	○	○	○	○
6	○	○	○	○	○	○	○
5	○	○	○	○	○	○	○
4	○	○	○	○	○	○	○
3	○	○	○	○	○	○	○
2	○	○	○	○	○	○	○
1	○	○	○	○	○	○	○

Date: _____

A Letter to My Future Self

_____

_____

_____

_____

_____

_____

_____

_____

_____

_____

_____

_____

_____

_____

_____

Notes

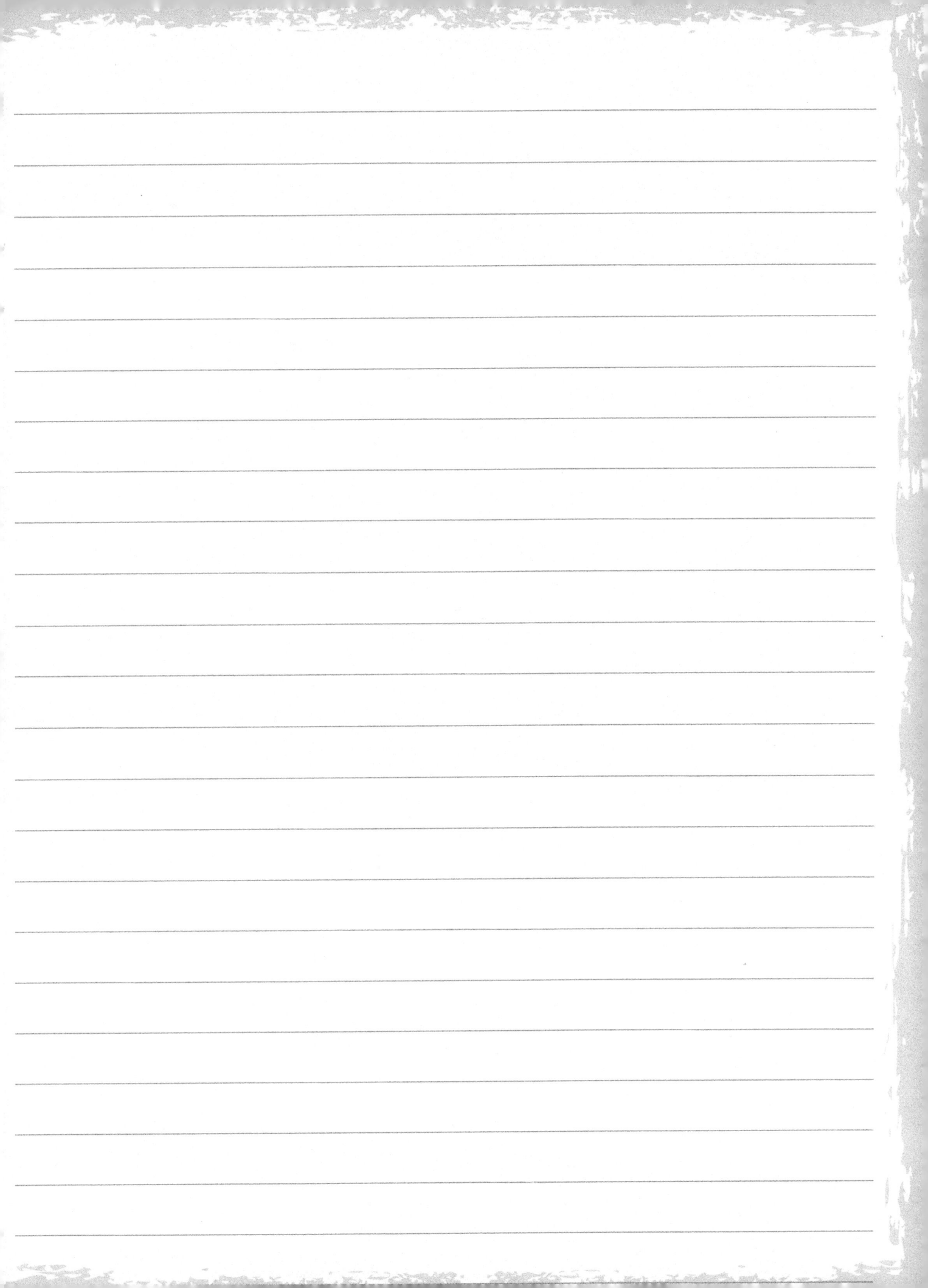

Ready to continue your journey with another? Here are some other books you might enjoy...

Procrastinate No More!: A practical Guide & Notebook to Help You Stop Procrastination When It Starts

Self-love Starts With Thank You: A 90-Day Prompt Journal to Boost Self-esteem

The Happy Plan: Plan Your Happiness, Track Your Results

Thank You to All My Haters: A 90-Day Unconventional Gratitude Journal

I Know I Can Freedom Planner and Journal: A 52-week planner & Journal for upcoming entrepreneurs, side hustlers, and freelancers

This workbook was brought to you by:
Mukaki Planners and Journals

Made in the USA
Las Vegas, NV
27 September 2021